Introduction

Purpose of SWYT Journal

Help you Locate, Reveal, and Strengthen Your (DNA)

Determined Natural Ability!

Today is the beginning of_____understanding How to become a better version of myself as often as I choose. I'm GIFTED Life with a certain amount of Time that belongs to me in moments, seconds, minutes, hours, days, weeks, months, and years. I commit to myself by following the processes within Stop Wasting Your Time Journal that I shall reveal the Valuable Well of Content I am to everyone who Chooses to interact with me. I also Understand that my Maximum personal growth to success is up to my willingness of habitual Mindset change as needed. My signature below on the bottom of this page confirms my New beginning to a more Focused person of wellness from within and without and my age does not define my Value.

Sincerely,

_____

New Beginning Date_____

Acknowledgement

Cynthia Johnson of www.dscpublishers.com
Publisher, editor, Graphic artist, Creative coordinator

SWYT

A Self-Reflection Journal

By Dr. M.E. Miller Sr.

SWYT
A Self-Reflection Journal

Dr. M.E. Miller Sr.

US Copyright © 2025 **CI-40726452558**

2nd Edition

All rights reserved. No part of this book may be reproduced or transmitted in any form or by any means without written permission from the author.

ISBN: **978-1-7337077-3-2**

Printed in the USA

SWYT Blueprint for discovery of your DNA - Determined Natural Ability

Everyone has the ability to Change lives. But the ability to Understand starts with visiting our Past Pain. You see our Past pain is the entry point to understanding our Value.

How do I know?

Because I have Lived the process 55 years prior to share how Pain is a Mine for growth, whether it's my pain or someone else. Your growth and change will be guided through questions. Let's begin.

SWYT

A Self-Reflection Journal

Month One

Who has hurt you from the past in life?

Write the details about the pain.

Do you think it was done on purpose or intentional?

_____

_____

_____

_____

Have you healed from the hurt? Yes or No

_____

If No, are you willing to be healed from the pain?

_____

If Yes, what process did you permit/allow to heal you?

_____

_____

_____

_____

_____

What are the benefits added to your daily living beyond the healing?

_____
_____
_____
_____
_____
_____
_____
_____

Are you sharing your story to help others move beyond their pain? Yes or No

_____

If Yes, where are you sharing your story to help others?

_____
_____
_____
_____
_____
_____

If no, why not?

_____
_____
_____
_____
_____

Write your reasons?

_____
_____
_____
_____
_____
_____
_____
_____
_____
_____
_____
_____

The formatted reminder process is below for becoming whole in life and thriving in living!

WHO - will you align with for healing?

_____
_____
_____
_____
_____
_____
_____
_____
_____
_____
_____
_____
_____
_____
_____

WHAT - will be your purpose to serve others?

WHERE - is the best place to begin?

WHY - is this most important to you?

WHEN - will you begin?

HOW - long do you intend to keep growing and developing yourself?

_____
_____
_____
_____
_____
_____
_____
_____
_____
_____
_____
_____
_____
_____
_____
_____
_____
_____

SWYT

A Self-Reflection Journal

Month Two

Who has hurt you from the past in life?

Write the details about the pain.

Do you think it was done on purpose or intentional?

_____
_____
_____
_____

Have you healed from the hurt? Yes or No

_____

If No, are you willing to be healed from the pain?

_____

If Yes, what process did you permit/allow to heal you?

_____
_____
_____
_____
_____
_____

What are the benefits added to your daily living beyond the healing?

_____
_____
_____
_____
_____
_____
_____

Are you sharing your story to help others move beyond their pain? Yes or No

_____

If Yes, where are you sharing your story to help others?

_____
_____
_____
_____
_____
_____

If no, why not?
_____
_____
_____
_____
_____

Write your reasons?
_____
_____
_____
_____
_____
_____
_____
_____
_____
_____
_____
_____

The formatted reminder process is below for becoming whole in life and thriving in living!

WHO - will you align with for healing?

_____
_____
_____
_____
_____
_____
_____
_____
_____
_____
_____
_____
_____
_____
_____

WHAT - will be your purpose to serve others?

WHERE - is the best place to begin?

WHY - is this most important to you?

WHEN - will you begin?

HOW - long do you intend to keep growing and developing yourself?

SWYT

A Self-Reflection Journal

Month Three

Who has hurt you from the past in life?

Write the details about the pain.

Do you think it was done on purpose or intentional?

_____
_____
_____
_____

Have you healed from the hurt? Yes or No

_____

If No, are you willing to be healed from the pain?

_____

If Yes, what process did you permit/allow to heal you?

_____
_____
_____
_____
_____
_____

What are the benefits added to your daily living beyond the healing?

_____
_____
_____
_____
_____
_____
_____
_____

Are you sharing your story to help others move beyond their pain? Yes or No

_____

If Yes, where are you sharing your story to help others?

_____
_____
_____
_____
_____
_____
_____

If no, why not?

_____
_____
_____
_____

Write your reasons?

_____
_____
_____
_____
_____
_____
_____
_____
_____
_____
_____

The formatted reminder process is below for becoming whole in life and thriving in living!

WHO - will you align with for healing?

_____
_____
_____
_____
_____
_____
_____
_____
_____
_____
_____
_____
_____
_____
_____

WHAT - will be your purpose to serve others?

WHERE - is the best place to begin?

WHY - is this most important to you?

WHEN - will you begin?

HOW - long do you intend to keep growing and developing yourself?

Prevention Maintenance

Well since you've made it this far in your development, you are receptive how to continue your growth for the rest of your life. The most simplistic way to maintain is through my Concept coaching Write, Rest, Reflect, Refine.

I would like to congratulate you for arriving to this level of Mindset.
I believe you understand the value you add to others that interact within the different realms of life. So, Write/record your thoughts, allow them to Rest, revisit them to Reflect, and because you do so, more content will be added in time and Refinement will be your resolve ongoing. Further content explanation of this Concept is available.

Prevention has been my empowerment for lifelong wholeness from pain.
Reflect intentionally upon each line and create a brief story of something that you can do more Refined, which allows individual day by day Growth.

Do this with each Acrostic Coaching below. Do not rush, take your time and GROW YOUR Mindset further.

When OUR Mind continue to renew, we continue to Grow and change others around us without saying one Word to them personally.

P roper preparation with Persistence

L eaves YOU

A n ADVANTAGE

N ever without OPTIONS

H elpful or HARMFUL

A ctions that

B ring

I NCREASE or decrease

T O YOUR LIFE!

G rant YOURSELF

O ptions that

A LLOW YOU Future

L everage to SUCCEED

**NOTE - Never think You ever arrived, there's always ROOM for GROWTH!

"When one thinks they have arrived, THEN BEGINS YOUR DEMISE"

Dr. Michael E. Miller, Sr
AKA - Mr. 1% Unlimited Thinker

Contacts

Website @ StopWastingYourTime.org

Calendar - Appointments
Contact - 813-406-3113

www.ingramcontent.com/pod-product-compliance
Lightning Source LLC
Chambersburg PA
CBHW030600080526
44585CB00012B/438